THE WORLD OF
DISASTERS

Ned Halley

KINGFISHER

KINGFISHER
Kingfisher Publications Plc
New Penderel House,
283–288 High Holborn,
London WC1V 7HZ
www.kingfisherpub.com

First published by Kingfisher Publications Plc 2005
10 9 8 7 6 5 4

4TR/1007/TIMS/PICA/128MA/F

A CIP catalogue record for this book is available
from the British Library.

ISBN-13: 978 0 7534 1074 5
ISBN-10: 0 7534 1074 5

Printed in China

Editor: Jonathan Stroud
Designer: Veneta Altham
Cover designer: Malcolm Parchment
Picture manager: Jane Lambert

First published as *The Best-Ever Book of Disasters*

CONTENTS

Canada
Ice storm, 1998

Missouri, USA
Tornado, 1925

NATURAL DISASTERS

It's a dangerous world. We try to make it safe for ourselves, but wild weather and violent geological events are simply beyond our control. When tornadoes or earthquakes strike populated places, they can spell disaster.

Are natural calamities more common now than they were in the past? News coverage can make it seem so, but it is not nature that's changing – it is us. Since 1900, the world's population has more than tripled, and the built-up areas have increased over five times in size. Regions prone to disastrous events are densely populated. Today, more than half of all people live in areas which are at constant risk of flooding.

Whether through optimism or necessity, people often ignore very real dangers. We crowd into huge cities, such as San Francisco and Tokyo, which we know

Europe
Pandemic, 1918

Pompeii, Italy
Volcano, AD79

Crete
Tsunami, 1500BC

Tokyo, Japan
Earthquake, 1923

China
Floods, 1998

Bangladesh
Floods, 1998

North Africa
Locusts, 1988

Krakatau, Indonesia
Volcano, 1883

Sydney, Australia
Bushfire, 1997

have suffered terrible earthquakes, and will almost certainly be struck again. Dangerous volcanic areas are populated too. When Vesuvius destroyed Pompeii in AD79, it killed about 2,000 people. If it erupted today – and it might – it would endanger a million lives.

However, it is true that our chances of surviving natural disaster are now much better. Satellite-aided weather forecasting and underground sensor systems can give warnings of imminent storms or seismic events. And much progress has been made against that unseen natural enemy – disease. The plagues that once brought disaster to whole nations can now be controlled by modern medicine. Or so we hope...

Krakatau

The volcanic eruption of Indonesia's Krakatau island on 27 August 1883 was the most violent explosion in history – up to 10,000 times the power of the first atomic bomb. The shock waves shook the entire planet and circled the globe seven times. The sound of the explosion sounded like the roar of heavy guns to people nearly 3,000km away and ash fell worldwide.

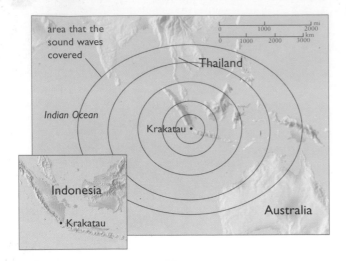

The biggest bang in history
The huge explosion was heard over one-twelfth of the surface of the Earth. Travelling at the speed of sound, it took two or more hours to reach Australia and Thailand – and four hours before it was heard on the island of Rodriguez, 4,800km to the west.

Tides of destruction

Krakatau was uninhabited, but 36,380 people on the surrounding islands were killed. Many were buried under millions of tonnes of burning rocks and ash hurled out by the blast. But most died in the 160 villages that were deluged by giant waves set off by the explosion. Tides caused by the waves snapped the anchor chains of ships moored at ports in Chile, on the far side of the world.

Darkness at noon
Ash from big eruptions forms dense clouds and can block out the Sun. This photograph was taken after the eruption of Mt Pinatubo in the Philippines in 1991 – at midday.

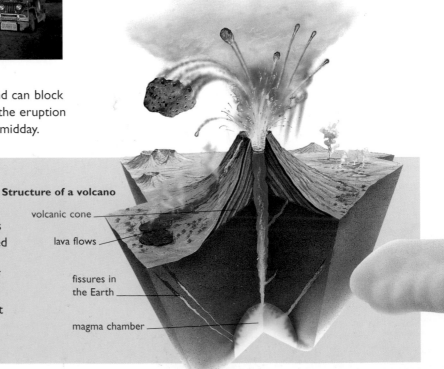

Pressure cooker
The first explosions in Krakatau's three-day eruption opened the volcano's magma chamber to the sea. Water rushed in through fissures, and reacted with molten rock to cause a huge build-up of steam-pressure. The resulting blast blew the mountain cone to pieces, hurling out red-hot rocks the size of houses.

Structure of a volcano
volcanic cone
lava flows
fissures in the Earth
magma chamber

Big blast
The Statue of Liberty,
which stands
80 metres high,
is shown to scale.

Fiery avalanche
The eruption blew Vesuvius' whole cone to smithereens, creating pyroclastic flows – avalanches of scorching ash and dust. With terrifying speeds of up to 160km/h, the flows rolled down the volcano's shattered slopes, straight into the town of Pompeii. People in the streets and houses were choked and burnt to death as they fled. Victims were quickly entombed in the ash, which continued to rain down for two days, burying everything to the depth of a two-storey building.

Vesuvius

In AD79, the Roman citizens of Pompeii were enjoying the good life. Their seaside town, said to have been founded 500 years earlier by the mythical hero Hercules, was famed for its beautiful art and buildings. Vineyards planted on the fertile slopes of nearby Mount Vesuvius made wines famous throughout Italy. But the mountain held a dark secret. In a gigantic eruption on 24 August, Vesuvius obliterated Pompeii.

Forgotten for 1,700 years
Pompeii disappeared under the ash and was later planted over with vineyards. Excavations only began in 1763, and have since uncovered most of the town, together with 2,000 of its citizens, frozen in time. Today, Pompeii provides a unique insight into the Roman world.

A dog's death
Bodies buried in the ash rotted away, leaving hollow cavities. Filled with plaster, these reveal victims, and their pets, in perfect detail.

A sea change
Pompeii was originally built next to the beach. The rock and ash ejected from Vesuvius filled up so much of the bay that the excavated town now stands 3km from the shore. In Roman times, the population was about 20,000, but today millions live in the shadow of the volcano.

Tokyo earthquake

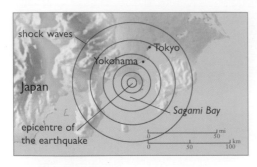

Sudden collapse

Measuring 8.2 on the Richter Scale, the quake's epicentre was in Sagami Bay, where the seabed dropped by 400 metres. Near Tokyo, the thriving seaport of Yokohama was also almost completely destroyed.

Before 1 September 1923, Japan's capital was home to 2.5 million people. Then it was struck by one of the most devastating earthquakes in history. The main shock came at midday, when families were cooking lunch. Charcoal burners were overturned, starting fires which spread rapidly among the close-packed timber houses. Half the city burned, and 142,000 people died. A million more, made homeless, moved away. Once the world's fifth largest city, Tokyo became the tenth.

A million homeless

More than 500,000 of Tokyo's flimsy wooden homes collapsed or burned in the raging fires. Earth tremors, which continued for days, broke up the underground water pipes, making fire-fighting impossible. People slept out of doors, afraid of being trapped under falling roofs. One eye-witness described the scene: "All day and all night, men, women and children walk the camps and parks searching for lost relatives."

Danger below

Tokyo stands near a fault line, one of the meeting-points of the moving continent-sized plates that form the Earth's crust. As the plates grind together, they release shock waves that are felt on the surface as violent tremors.

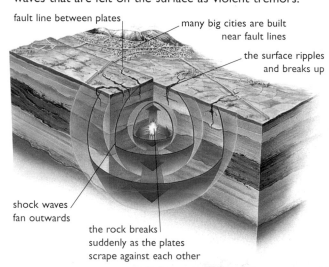

fault line between plates

many big cities are built near fault lines

the surface ripples and breaks up

shock waves fan outwards

the rock breaks suddenly as the plates scrape against each other

An ever-present risk

Even with the latest construction methods, cities still face destruction today. The devastating 1995 earthquake at Kobe, 400km southwest of Tokyo, caused US$10 billion in damage, killed 5,391 people and left another 310,000 homeless.

Coast to coast
An eruption on Santorini, 130km to the north, caused the tsunami. Crete stood directly in the way of the huge waves that deluged coasts across the Mediterranean.

Tsunami

Imagine looking out to sea from a sunny beach. Something is wrong. The tide is going out – and not coming back. All the way to the horizon, the sea floor is revealed. Fish flop helplessly, boats are stranded. And now comes the great wave. With a thunderous, deafening roar, it rears up like a moving mountain, crashing ashore with unimaginable force.

The drowning of an empire

The tsunami that struck the Mediterranean island of Crete around 1500BC was one of the greatest natural disasters in history. The colossal 60-metre-high waves swept across the entire island, drowning the Minoan civilization – the oldest and richest in Europe. The destruction of this kingdom is the likely basis for the legend of the Lost City of Atlantis.

Waves of destruction

The word 'tsunami' comes from Japan, where 'harbour waves' are a constant danger. The 10-metre-high giants that crashed into Okushiri Island on 13 July 1993, caused widespread devastation, killing more than 200 people.

Ocean racers

1. Undersea earthquakes and eruptions cause massive falls and rises in the ocean floor, convulsing the sea into great wave movements.

2. The waves, 1,000km or more wide, cause the entire sea level to rise. In open sea, they travel faster than a bullet speeding from a gun.

3. Near land, friction with the rising seabed slows the tsunami. The sea is sucked from the shore into the wave, making it rear up as it hits.

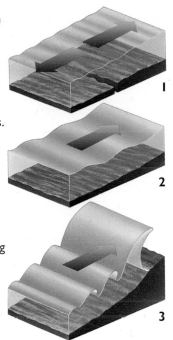

Ice storm

Frozen solid
Freezing rain is different from hail or snow. Each drop is a water-filled ice bomb, exploding on contact with a cold surface and freezing instantly into a hard, clear glaze of ice.

Canada is accustomed to the cold, but the storm of January 1998 caused a national emergency. Freezing rain clamped provinces such as Quebec and Ontario under a mantle of ice. Heat and lighting were cut off and the country's economy shut down, as millions were stranded in their freezing homes. Over 11,000 troops were mobilized to help restore power – the biggest military call-up in Canada's peacetime history.

Ice can build up dangerously on the wings of aircraft flying through clouds of freezing rain.

The only safe place is inside, although wrecked pylons may cut off electric heat and light.

Freezing rain forms a glaze on pavements, making them far too slippery to walk on.

Roads covered by thick ice can be impossible to drive on.

Trees and pylons, coated with layers of ice, collapse under the enormous weight.

Cars and machinery left exposed are soon frozen solid.

Thick coat
Water falling as freezing rain turns to ice on impact. It can quickly build up to thicknesses of 10cm, damaging property and killing farm livestock in minutes. Insured losses in Canada's freeze came to a massive $1.2 billion.

Deadly hazards of ice
Only a few people were found frozen to death during the storm, but many more died from carbon monoxide poisoning as they tried to keep warm with poorly ventilated home-made heaters made from barbecues. More were later reported killed by falling icicles during the thaw.

Toppled by the weight

Layers of ice enlarge electricity cables to
three times their usual width, dragging
down the steel pylons supporting them.
At Drummondsville, south of Montreal,
a series of eight giant pylons collapsed,
blacking out 482,000 homes in the city.
The ice storm raged for six days, but
it took weeks to restore power to the
millions left freezing in unlit houses
at temperatures as low as minus 27°C.

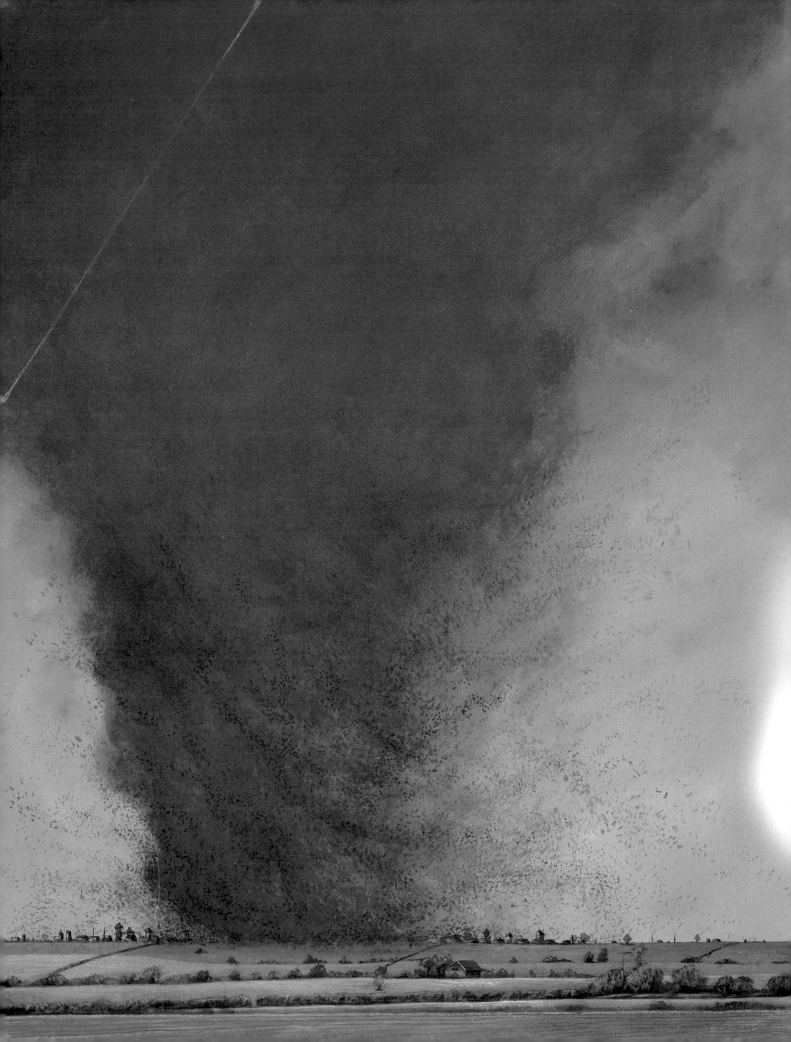

Twister

It emerged from thunderclouds over the state of Missouri, USA, at 1pm on 18 March 1925. Over the next three hours, the longest-lasting and most destructive tornado in history ploughed through ten towns. At times over 1km wide and moving faster than a speeding car, the twister smashed thousands of homes and killed 689 people.

debris flung into the air is a major cause of casualties

homes in tornado black spots often have cellars for refuge

houses burst apart

wind speeds can exceed 100 metres per second

Brewing up a storm

Tornadoes are violent thunderstorms, caused when warm, wet air is drawn up from the ground and meets colder air moving down. The opposing draughts combine in a corkscrew motion, sending a violently spinning funnel of air plunging down to the ground.

Merciless killer

The most powerful twisters smash and grab everything in their way. Buildings, vehicles and even the ground itself are sucked up into their vortices. The bodies of people caught up in the 1925 storm were hurled 1.5km from its path.

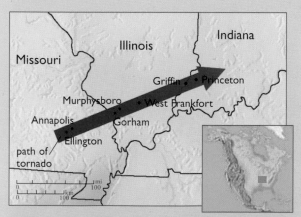

Trail of devastation

The 1925 tornado raced 350km across the USA.

• Appearing at Ellington, Missouri, at 1pm, it took 15 minutes to destroy nearby Annapolis.

• Travelling northeast at 100km/hr, it ripped into Illinois state.

• In Murphysboro, 234 people died and 40 percent of the town was destroyed.

• The tornado subsided at 4.30pm, after hitting Princeton, Indiana.

Torn apart

Buildings in the path of a tornado often look as if they have exploded. Twisters tear at solid structures like a pair of giant hands wrenching savagely in opposite directions.

Bushfire

On 2 December 1997, Australia's greatest city faced catastrophe. Fires raging in bushland on three sides of Sydney suddenly swept into the suburbs. Before firefighters could gain control, dozens of houses were destroyed. The flames, whipped up by high winds, lit the night sky over the city as 5,000 emergency workers battled hundreds of separate fires. Only their courage, and a quick weather change, prevented an even worse disaster.

Spreads like wildfire

In Australia's tinder-dry bush, fires are easily started – by lightning, arson, or even from the Sun's rays magnified through the glass of a carelessly discarded bottle. Blazes spread at speeds of up to 2km a *minute*. The fires around Sydney reached to within 20km of the centre, leaving the city darkened by a pall of choking smoke and fumes. Many homes were evacuated until the danger was past.

Street in flames
As Australia's fast-growing cities expand further into the surrounding countryside, the danger from bushfires increases. The 1997 blaze burnt out most of this street in the Sydney suburb of Menai.

Fighting fire with fire
Firebreaks help to stop the spread of a blaze in woodland. All the trees are felled and bulldozers clear the wood to the side of the break nearest the approaching flames. This material is then set alight to widen the firebreak.

Bombing the blazes

Bush and forest fires can be fought from the air. Highly skilled pilots skim the aircraft over open water, scooping tonnes of it up into special tanks in the fuselage. The load is then released, like a bomb, on to the fire below.

Pandemic

"The deadliest killer in human history" is how scientists now describe the influenza virus of 1918. In six months it killed between 20 and 40 million people in a pandemic – a global epidemic – and then vanished. Unlike bubonic plague (the Black Death) which can now be controlled by modern medicine, flu has no known cure. If a similar virus broke out again, it could be the greatest disaster ever to strike humankind.

Flimsy protection

In 1918, people did not know how the deadly flu spread. Millions wore masks in the hope of avoiding infection when out in public places, but the gauze offered no real protection against the microscopic virus.

Worsened by war

The virus struck towards the end of World War I (1914–18), killing twice as many people as the war itself. It was first called 'Spanish flu', although it probably started in China. It reached Europe from the USA, carried by American servicemen aboard crowded troopships. In the filthy, wet trenches of the war zones, it spread like wildfire, mostly attacking young adults and causing death from lung infection, often within hours.

Hopeless cases

Emergency hospitals were set up to isolate patients in the hope of limiting the flu's spread. But there was no effective treatment, and victims who developed pneumonia as a complication were likely to die, literally drowning from the fluid filling their lungs. The antibiotics used today to combat pneumonia were not discovered until 1933. The spread of the virus could not be controlled either – ships carried it to every part of the globe, and by early 1919, nearly half the world's 1.8 billion people had been infected.

A plague's progress

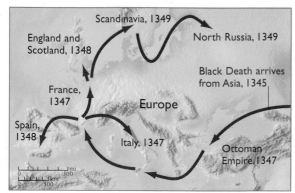

The Black Death of 1347–52 spread to Europe from the East. Carried by rats and transmitted to humans by fleas, the plague killed around 25 million people, reducing the population of some countries by a third.

Grim reaper

The Black Death was a horrific bacterial disease that brought almost certain death. Its name came from the black, blood-filled swellings seen beneath victims' skin. So many people died that carts piled with corpses were a common sight in towns and villages. Many medieval people saw the plague as a punishment from God. Paintings of the time depict Death as a skeleton riding a cart over the bodies of victims, rich and poor alike.

Locust

The swarm is vast. It blocks out the Sun. As many as 50 billion ravenously hungry insects are on the move. As the sinister black cloud, 50km long, passes over green fields, it suddenly wheels and descends with the deafening beat of countless wings. Minutes later, thousands of tonnes of crops have been devoured. All across Africa, in the summer of 1988, people faced famine because of an old enemy – the locust plague.

Danger in numbers
The African migratory locust is only 5cm long, but in its adult, winged state it can fly up to 5,000km between breeding cycles. Each time the swarm feeds, females lay hundreds of eggs, swelling the numbers of locusts by 100 times or more.

1. The wet winter of 1987-88 in Mali and Mauritania was ideal for locust breeding.

2. Early in 1988, the swarms moved north to devastate crops in Morocco and Algeria.

3. By June, the swarm had eaten 1m tonnes of crops in Chad, Niger and Sudan.

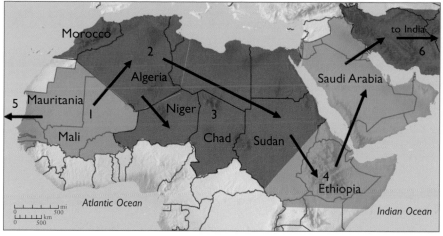

4. Swarms then spread southeast to Ethiopia, reaching Saudi Arabia in autumn 1988.

5. In October, a swarm was blown 5,000km across the Atlantic, a record flight of 5 days.

6. In 1989, a swarm of locusts reached India, almost 10,000km from the first breeding area.

Halfway around the world
In 1988, North Africa enjoyed exceptionally good crops of vital cereals such as maize. But the wet weather was also ideal for locusts. Swarms were blown by prevailing winds right across the continent. Some even spread across the Atlantic and to India.

Alone in the desert
In the dry conditions usual in Africa, locusts are solitary creatures. They live like ordinary grasshoppers and are a dull, sandy colour, which camouflages them from predators in the desert.

On the march
If rain comes, locusts feast on the fresh greenery and breed rapidly. The young become brightly coloured to identify each other as they crowd together, hopping many kilometres to feed.

Ready for take-off
If the weather stays wet and food remains plentiful, the hoppers mature into their adult, winged form. They continue breeding, and soon the first large swarms fly off to hunt for food.

A perpetual menace
Modern pesticides have done little to reduce the locust threat. The 1988 swarms, the most devastating for 30 years, spread across half of Africa, even though the United Nations spent $240 million on spraying. The best control method is to treat locusts while they are immature 'hoppers' foraging in great numbers on the ground. On the wing, swarms can be attacked only from aircraft, which spray the insects from above.

Biting back
For thousands of years, locusts have provided a plentiful source of food for birds, animals – and humans. These people in Morocco have collected a large harvest, ready to be fried or grilled, and eaten like prawns. Delicious!

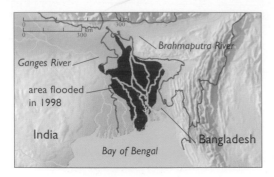

A nation under water

Bangladesh's population has grown from 80 million to about 140 million since independence in 1971. Most people live in the flood-plains and deltas of the Ganges and Brahmaputra rivers, where fertile soil means good harvests, but floods regularly cover half the entire country.

Living on the edge

More than half the people on Earth live in places where floods are a constant danger. It's not as crazy as it sounds, because land regularly flooded by rivers is particularly fertile for farming. But the price can be terrible. The flood-plains of the Ganges River in Bangladesh and the Yangtze River in China are two of the world's most heavily populated areas. In 1998, over two-thirds of Bangladesh was submerged and 10 million people were made homeless. Calamity came too in China, where the Yangtze stranded millions more.

dykes are built higher as the river level rises

land is formed by mud deposits left by floods

farmers prosper from the rich soil's harvest

as the river drops sediment, its bed becomes much higher than the land around

The gift of the river

Over thousands of years, rivers like the Yangtze in China have created fertile farmland, leaving layers of rich silt behind as they flood and then retreat. To protect their fields from severe flooding, farmers build giant dykes of earth. These are reinforced by long nets woven from local crops and filled with stones.

In the breach

Dykes have guarded China's farmland for centuries, and are often big enough to take roads along their tops. But sudden rises in water levels can still cause disaster. After months of rain in 1998, the Yangtze burst through. More than 700,000 rescuers, including thousands of soldiers, struggled to save the dykes – but over a million people lost their homes.

From feast to famine

Living in a flood zone is a balancing act. The fertile land enables farmers to reap two or three harvests a year. But in disasters such as the Bangladesh floods of 1998, families face cruel hardships when rivers overflow. Their homes and fields are flooded, drowning the crops and leaving them buried under a new layer of mud. Then they are faced with months of food and medical shortages before the waters finally subside.

MAN-MADE DISASTERS

Alaskan coast
Oil spill, 1989 ▲

The disasters we bring
upon ourselves are caused by
human error, incompetence and
misfortune. Often they arise from
a mixture of these – the famous
sinking of *Titanic*, for example, is
a story of simple over-confidence
and sheer bad luck. Other cases stem
from a series of small mishaps, none
seemingly important on their own. The
terrible air crash at Tenerife happened because
mistake piled on to mistake until disaster struck.

New York, USA
Wall Street Crash, 1929 ▲

North Atlantic
Titanic, 1912 ▲

The worst disasters, on the other
hand, happen when clear warnings
have been ignored – as they
were when operators shut
down safety systems at
the Chernobyl nuclear
reactor. Engineers
knew it was
dangerous,
but they

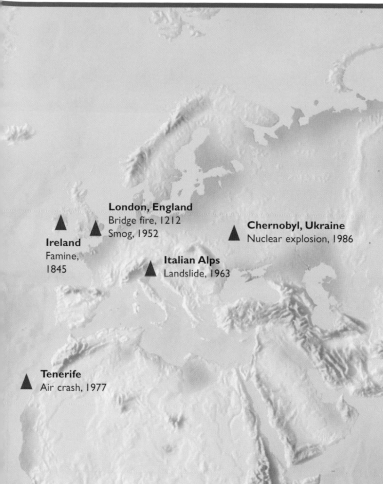

Ireland
Famine,
1845

London, England
Bridge fire, 1212
Smog, 1952

Italian Alps
Landslide, 1963

Chernobyl, Ukraine
Nuclear explosion, 1986

Tenerife
Air crash, 1977

Tragedies of our own making
Triumphs of human technology allow construction of great cities, fast transport and powerful machines. Yet with every achievement, there is the potential for calamity, if people grow careless or luck runs out. This map shows some of the most notable man-made disasters, which are featured in this section.

But man-made disasters have costs that are not always measured in loss of human life. The Wall Street Crash killed no one, but led to a worldwide depression in which tens of millions lost their livelihoods. Increasingly important, too, are environmental catastrophes. The *Exxon Valdez* oil spill and the Great London Smog are only two examples of the devastation that has been wrought worldwide by humankind's carelessness with modern resources.

carried on because they were used to obeying orders. The tragedy was that no one had the courage to say no to the experiment before it was too late.

Thankfully, such major calamities are rare events. In some areas, things are actually getting safer – the number of people killed each year in aircraft accidents has not risen since the 1950s, even though there are now over one billion passenger journeys taken every year.

Famine

It was a national tragedy. By the 1840s, half the people of Ireland depended on just one food – the potato. It gave them most of the nutrients they needed, and many had stopped planting any other crop. Then, without warning, a new disease infected the potato plants, wiping out the harvest for years. In the famine that followed, a million Irish people died of starvation and sickness.

Grim harvest

Potato blight turned the crop into a black, evil-smelling slime. The disease, like the potato itself, came from America, reaching Ireland in the summer of 1845. It spread rapidly, until Ireland's reliance on this single 'miracle' crop – one man could plant enough plants to feed 40 people for a year – became a disaster.

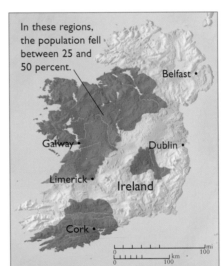

In these regions, the population fell between 25 and 50 percent.

Belfast •
Galway •
Dublin •
Limerick •
Ireland
Cork •

Blighted land

In the three generations from 1785 to 1845, the Irish population had grown by three times, rising from 2.8 to 8.3 million. When the blight struck, millions died or emigrated, and the population plummeted. Even after the famine ended, poverty forced people to leave. Today, Ireland is home to only four million people.

Perilous crossing

Driven from the land, 1.2 million Irish people emigrated in 1847–52, most of them to the United States. The long voyage in crowded, unsanitary ships was a dangerous one – among every 100 passengers, 16 would die at sea.

Help from above

Today, famine continues to stalk many countries, especially in Africa, where food shortages due to crop failure can turn into disaster because of warfare or corruption. Then, international agencies must bring in emergency food by every means available.

Uncharitable response

Ireland, then a province of the United Kingdom, was largely owned by English landlords, some of whom reacted to famine by turning tenants off their land when they could not pay the rent. People who refused to leave were evicted by the army, who often burned their homes to ensure they would not return. The British government did provide some aid to Ireland – but it was too little, too late.

Chernobyl

In April 1986, the world held its breath. Live television pictures from the Soviet Union showed there had been an explosion at Chernobyl nuclear power station. A reactor, burning out of control, was belching tonnes of radioactive materials into the air. Soviet officials admitted to 31 deaths, but evacuated 135,000 people. Unknown numbers have since died from radiation sickness.

Raining uranium
During what the Soviet authorities called 'an unauthorized experiment' by staff, Reactor No. 4 exploded at 1.23am on 26 April. White-hot radioactive fuel fragments landed all over the power station, starting fires near other reactors. Local firemen risked their lives to enter the area and put out the flames.

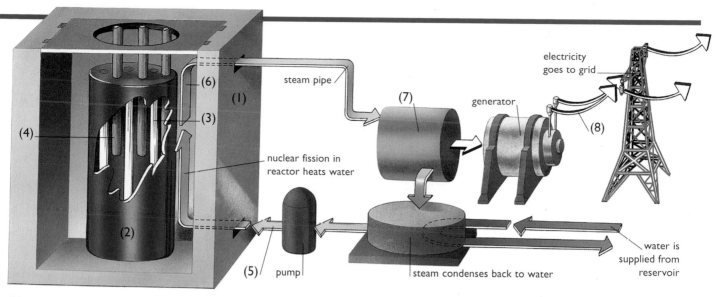

electricity goes to grid

steam pipe

(7)

generator

(8)

nuclear fission in reactor heats water

(5) pump

steam condenses back to water

water is supplied from reservoir

How a reactor works

Nuclear reactors harness heat-energy produced by fission, the violent splitting of uranium atoms. The heat is used to generate electricity. Inside a concrete vessel (1), the reactor core (2) contains uranium fuel rods (3) and control rods (4) which are raised and lowered to control the rate of fission.

To cool the reactor, cold water is pumped in (5), and the reactor's heat turns the water to steam (6). The steam turns a turbine (7) to generate electricity (8). At Chernobyl, operators cut off the steam to see if the turbine would turn on its own. But it slowed at once, reducing power to the water pumps cooling the reactor, which instantly overheated violently.

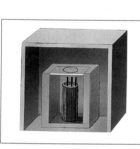

Sweden

spread of cloud after four days

Soviet Union

Kiev • Chernobyl

Europe

spread of cloud after eleven days

Africa

Bad vibrations

In seconds, the heat of the reactor had reached dangerous levels. But its automatic cooling system had been shut off and the control rods had been pulled up to increase power. Strong vibrations now made it impossible to lower the rods to cool the reactor.

Reaction force

The uncontrolled rise in reactor output began to melt the fuel rods. Uranium leaked into the cooling water, creating high pressure steam and gases. These exploded, blowing the 2,000-tonne roof off the reactor and out through the main building. The second explosion followed as the outside air came into contact with the reactor core.

Slow burner

The core burned for two weeks, sending tonnes of radioactive ash and dust into the outside air.

A deadly cloud

The first fallout was detected in Sweden on 28 April. Winds and rain carried the dust cloud over Europe, contaminating farm produce for years. The Chernobyl reactor was finally buried under 5,000 tonnes of clay and sand, and sealed in a concrete tomb.

Cleaning action

Radioactive dust fell thickly on towns near the reactor, including Kiev, 120km away, where streets had to be hosed down. At Chernobyl itself, trees were felled, but could not be burned in case the smoke carried the poison back into the air. Everything, even the topsoil, was finally buried in deep, concrete-lined pits.

31

Bridge on fire

On a blustery day in July 1212, fires broke out on London Bridge – at both ends. Sweeping through the thatched buildings, the flames trapped the crowds crossing the bridge along its narrow street. In the panic, about 3,000 people were burned or crushed to death, or drowned in the Thames River below. The fire spread, and most of the city was destroyed in a disaster far worse than London's 'Great Fire' of 1666 – in which only six lives were lost.

Fighting force
In cities today, dedicated fire-fighters can control even the most serious blaze. But it was only in the 19th century that the first full-time fire brigades were established. By then, many of the world's cities, including New York, Rome and Moscow, had been largely destroyed by fire at least once.

Demolition gangs

In the Middle Ages, there were no water hoses, so water could only be carried in buckets. To prevent the spread of fire between streets, some timber-framed houses were pulled down by teams using hooks attached to long poles and chains. This created a big gap across which the flames could not leap.

Safety measures

After the 1212 disaster, London introduced its first fire-prevention laws. Roofs thatched with highly flammable straw or rushes were banned in favour of stone tiles, and every district had to have its own set of hooks for pulling down buildings in an emergency.

Spanning the centuries

Built in the 1170s, the 300-metre London Bridge was home to hundreds of families. It was a shopping street as well as a vital thoroughfare, with a drawbridge and gatehouse at either end, and a chapel in the middle. Although the houses were all destroyed in 1212, the stone piers survived, and the bridge remained an important crossing for another 600 years.

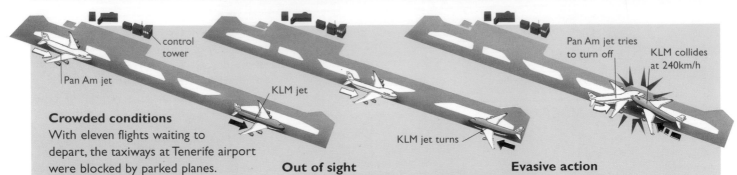

Crowded conditions
With eleven flights waiting to depart, the taxiways at Tenerife airport were blocked by parked planes. Aircraft were using the runway itself to taxi to the take-off point. Just before 5pm, the KLM 747 set off down the runway for the starting position, followed by the American Pan Am jet.

Out of sight
At the end of the runway, the KLM jumbo turned for take-off. In the dense fog, the pilot could not see the Pan Am jet straight ahead. He mistakenly believed he had permission to take off.

Evasive action
The moment the Pan Am pilot saw the approaching 747, he veered left to get off the runway. But, at 5.07pm, as the KLM jet left the ground, it crashed into the Pan Am's side.

Runway collision

One of the world's worst air disasters happened on the ground. On 27 March 1977, the fog-bound airport on the Spanish island of Tenerife was busy with flights diverted by a terrorist bomb blast from nearby Las Palmas. In a series of misunderstandings between the control tower and the crews of two jets – a Dutch KLM and an American Pan Am – the two aircraft collided on the runway, killing 583.

Flying blind
The Pan Am pilot recalled: "We saw lights ahead of us in the fog. At first we thought it was the KLM standing at the end of the runway. Then we realized they were coming towards us." Only just airborne, the Dutch plane ploughed into the Pan Am jet, then plunged to earth, where it exploded into flames.

Few survivors

Unseen from the control tower in the fog, the KLM jumbo was completely burnt out, killing all 248 on board. The crash's only survivors were those who managed to escape the stricken Pan Am jet before it too was destroyed by fire. Of the 634 people on board the planes, all but 51 died.

Fatal misunderstanding

The KLM pilot may have misheard a vital radio message from the control tower. He was not given take-off permission, but radio interference possibly confused the ground controller's instruction, "OK. Stand-by for take-off", as "OK ... for take-off". The lack of ground radar (now used in all major airports) meant controllers could not 'see' that the two planes were on a collision course.

Titanic

It should never have happened. On the night of 14 April 1912, the captain of the world's largest luxury liner knew he was in dangerous waters. In spite of ice warnings from ships nearby in the Atlantic, *Titanic* was sailing at close to top speed. At 11.40pm, ice was sighted dead ahead. The 46,000-tonne ship smashed into the iceberg, buckling the plates of her hull so that the water poured in. In under three hours, she was gone, and more than 1,500 people with her.

Collision course

It was a calm, clear night, but the dark mass of the iceberg blended in with the black sea. As soon as the danger came into view, the lookouts in the crow's nest above the foredeck rang the warning bell and phoned the bridge, "Iceberg, right ahead!" But it was too late.

Minutes from the end

Lights still blazed when the liner, taller than a ten-storey building, finally upended and broke in half. It was 2am, just 75 minutes after the first lifeboat had been lowered half-empty. At that time, many passengers refused to believe that the ship could sink. Now all the boats were gone and more than 1,000 people remained on board. "We could see groups clinging in clusters or bunches, like swarming bees," recalled one survivor, "only to fall in masses, pairs or singly, as the great part of the ship rose into the sky."

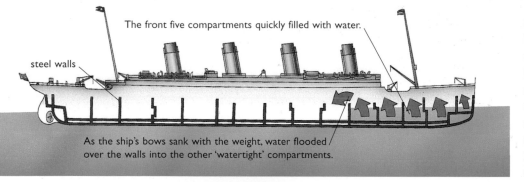

The front five compartments quickly filled with water.

steel walls

As the ship's bows sank with the weight, water flooded over the walls into the other 'watertight' compartments.

Damage beyond control

Below decks, *Titanic* was divided into compartments. If the ship was holed, only one section would flood. But the iceberg ruptured five at once. As the weight of the seawater dragged down the liner's bows, the front of the hull was rapidly flooded.

Wasted lives

The last lifeboat to be launched – seen here from the liner *Carpathia*, the first ship to the rescue – was almost full. But in the confusion, many lifeboats had been lowered with empty seats, costing as many as 500 people their chance of survival. Of 2,223 on board, only 492 passengers and 214 crew escaped.

Oil spill

"Evidently we are leaking some oil." This message came from the captain of the giant supertanker *Exxon Valdez*. His 200,000-tonne ship had run aground only hours after taking on a full load at the oil terminal in Prince William Sound, Alaska, USA. It was Good Friday, 24 March 1989. By Easter Monday, 10 million gallons of crude oil had spilled into the sea. It was one of the worst environmental disasters in history.

Circling the spill
Because oil is lighter than water and floats on the surface, inflatable tubes called booms are used to prevent slicks from spreading. The boom is reeled out from a ship to trap the slick in a loop. The oil can then be pumped from the surface into tankers.

Human failing
The *Exxon Valdez* disaster was caused by a simple navigational error. After leaving the port of Valdez, the crew changed course to avoid floating ice. They then failed to resume the usual course and struck a reef. The captain was asleep at the time. Investigators later found that he had been drinking, and had entrusted the steering to an inexperienced steersman.

Widespread pollution
Tides carried the spilled oil over 2,500km of Alaska's southern coastline, an area of great, unspoiled beauty. Clean-up work was seriously delayed as companies and officials argued over who would have to pay for it.

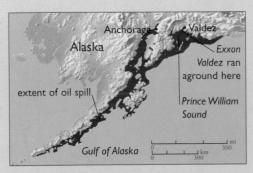

The cost to the region's wildlife was devastating. Ten years later, some species were still struggling to regain their numbers.

Many of the killer whale pods in Alaskan waters disappeared after the disaster.

Hundreds of cormorants were killed. Their populations have not yet recovered.

Mussels, an essential food for both birds and otters, were badly polluted by the spill.

Rare sea otters had been growing in numbers, but the oil spill killed thousands.

Salmon fishing was stopped to prevent the contaminated fish reaching the shops.

Common seaweed, vital to all coastal ecosystems, was severely affected.

The blackened shore

Cleaning up the *Exxon Valdez* spill took years and cost an incredible £12.5 billion. On shore, some teams used high-pressure hoses to dislodge the oil. Others simply shovelled it up from the beaches and carried it away in buckets. But oil clings like glue to everything it touches – especially fur and feathers. In Alaska, it killed at least 580,000 seabirds and 5,500 sea and river otters. The breeding grounds of countless seals, sealions, fish and birds were contaminated, and research into the long-term effects on Alaska's uniquely precious wildlife is still continuing today.

Helping hands
Volunteers flocked to Alaska to help with the huge task of rescuing oiled birds and animals. The disaster's one good outcome followed disputes over who should pay for the clean-up. The world's oil companies and shipowners agreed the Valdez Principles, which will ensure they take responsibility for oil spills in the future.

Smog

It is a blend of smoke and fog, a choking mixture of man-made pollution and natural mist, which settles over cities with potentially fatal results. In London, then the world's largest city, the Great Smog of 1952 killed 4,000 people in four days – and twice that number died later from its effects. After years of ignoring the problem, the government was forced to introduce tough clean-air laws. Despite the lessons learnt, smog remains a serious hazard in cities across the world today.

Stacks of smoke
Fifty years ago, Western nations depended on coal fires and coal-burning power stations, which all emitted filthy smoke. Many fuels are now cleaner, but increased burning worldwide means that pollution continues.

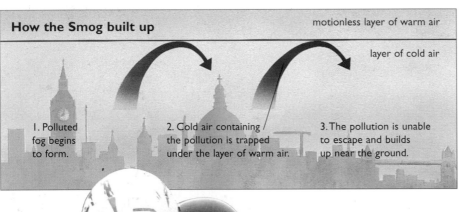

How the Smog built up

motionless layer of warm air

layer of cold air

1. Polluted fog begins to form.

2. Cold air containing the pollution is trapped under the layer of warm air.

3. The pollution is unable to escape and builds up near the ground.

Cold trap
Built in the low-lying London basin of the Thames River, Britain's capital has always been prone to the fog that forms as warm air condenses over cold ground. On 4 December 1952, a 'temperature inversion' occurred, when polluted cold air was trapped under a static layer of warm air. With no wind to shift it, the poisonous smog lingered until 9 December before finally clearing.

Not so clean air
City-dwellers in the Far East now commonly wear protection against pollution. In the Malaysian capital Kuala Lumpur, smoke from forest fires has combined with industrial and traffic fumes to make the air so dangerous that police are issued with masks. In the USA, cities such as Los Angeles have levels of dangerous fumes 400 times higher than the USA's Clean Air Act allows.

Thick as pea soup

At times during the Great Smog, visibility in London was less than one metre. Buses, ambulances and fire engines had to be led through the streets by guides carrying flares, and people got lost only metres from their own homes. The air, laden with filthy carbon and sulphur dioxide, turned the yellow-green colour that Londoners knew as 'a pea-souper'. Up to ten times heavier than normal air, the smog was lethal to people with heart or lung problems.

Landslide

Spanning a steep river gorge in the Italian Alps, the Vaiont Dam was the second highest in the world – and the most dangerous. Rockfalls were common in the region, and experts warned that the reservoir created by the dam could cause the submerged mountainsides to collapse. But the project went ahead. On 9 October 1963, the worst happened. A huge avalanche plunged into the lake, sending millions of tonnes of water over the dam and down into the heavily populated valley below.

Like an earthquake

The landslide hit the reservoir's floor with an impact that was felt all over Europe. The mountainous movement generated a rush of air so violent that it lifted the roofs from houses for miles around, and blew out windows and doors. Incredibly, the dam survived, but the vast body of water that surged over its top formed a 70-metre-high wave which swept away everything in its path, leaving more than 2,000 people dead.

Moving mountain

At 10.41pm, a 2km-wide strip of Mount Toc, the reservoir's south bank, collapsed. It filled half the lake, displacing 240 million cubic metres of water. The torrent sent over the dam destroyed most of the town of Longarone and several villages. At the lake's east end, hundreds more homes were deluged by waves from the impact.

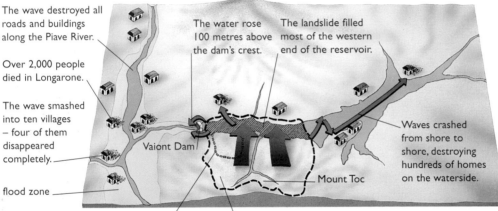

The wave destroyed all roads and buildings along the Piave River.

Over 2,000 people died in Longarone.

The wave smashed into ten villages – four of them disappeared completely.

flood zone

Vaiont Dam

The water rose 100 metres above the dam's crest.

The landslide filled most of the western end of the reservoir.

Waves crashed from shore to shore, destroying hundreds of homes on the waterside.

Mount Toc

This dotted area shows a major slide of just three years previously, which the dam's builders had ignored.

In under 30 seconds, a gigantic section of Mount Toc plummeted into the reservoir.

Snowed under

Avalanches are a constant hazard in mountain ranges such as the Alps in Central Europe. The risk of disastrous snowfalls increases in farming regions and ski resorts where mountainsides have been cleared of the trees which help to stabilize ground snow.

After the event

A priest prays over a victim of the Vaiont damburst. Many of the dead were unidentified, as no one from their villages survived to name them. The dam, built to generate hydro-electricity, had been in full operation for only a few months – following years of delay due to doubts about possible danger from landslides.

Mounds of worthless cash

Inflation – when money loses its value – can be a financial disaster. After World War I, 'hyperinflation' in Germany reduced the value of its currency, the mark, to virtually nothing. Germany had to pay huge sums in compensation to countries it had attacked in the war, but the government cheated by printing new bank notes to pay with. People lost faith in the worth of this money and the mark's value plummeted. In 1918, a loaf of bread cost one mark. In early 1923, the price had risen to 250 marks. By Christmas, it was 200 *billion* marks. Workers took their wages home in wheelbarrows, and children played with stacks of worthless notes. This economic anarchy lasted until the government introduced a new currency.

Wall Street Crash

The peace and welfare of every nation depend on its economic security. But that security is not guaranteed. Financial disasters can create mass poverty – as happened in the USA after the stock market crash of 24 October 1929. Share prices fell so low that many companies became worthless. Investors lost their money and businesses went bankrupt. With the country engulfed by depression, millions lost their jobs, then their homes. They went on the road in search of work, dependent on charity for survival. Countless numbers died from starvation and illness.

Standing in line

As the Great Depression gripped the United States, jobless numbers reached 14 million and average incomes halved. Americans, receiving no unemployment benefit, relied on soup kitchens – or begging – to stay alive. Recovery only began after a new president, Franklin D. Roosevelt, introduced the 'New Deal' in 1933. This helped the poor find food, shelter and work through community projects, building roads, dams and houses.

Hard times for farmers

In 1932, with the Depression at its height, America suffered another economic disaster. After years of good harvests from the great wheat-growing plains of the south, the vast region was struck by a severe drought. The land soon became a 'dust bowl'. Farmers lost their properties and moved into crude shacks. Half a million people abandoned their land before the drought ended – five long years later.

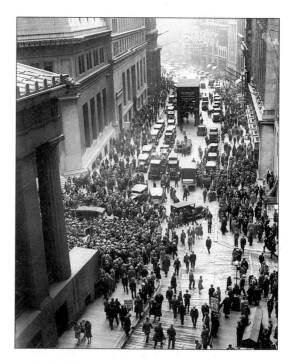

Panic in the street

On the morning of the great crash, the Stock Exchange in New York's Wall Street was a scene of chaos. Large investors were selling shares in response to fears about the worldwide economy. As news of the falling prices spread, thousands of small investors ordered their stockbrokers to sell 'at any price'. Panic broke out as the brokers failed to find any buyers. Millions of shares worth billions of dollars became entirely worthless in a matter of hours.

FUTURE DISASTERS

Is life on Earth becoming more dangerous? In one very important sense, it is. Global population is now 100 times greater than 500 years ago, and it is increasing at a frightening rate. Millions more people are now exposed to natural disasters, and the upsurge in population puts pressure on the quality of people's life across the globe. Many cities now face poverty, epidemics, overcrowding and rising crime.

Meanwhile, human technology causes increasing damage to Earth's environment. By stripping away the forests that once covered much of the land, and by polluting the atmosphere with industrial waste and transport fumes, we have begun the process of global warming. This is already leading to an increase in violent weather and flooding – and the risk that the ice caps could melt, drowning much of the world.

Technology has made our lives safer. New medicines can combat diseases that were once untreatable. But final triumph over illness is a long way off. Some diseases can be controlled, but none are eradicated.

Another threat comes from space. Giant meteorites have struck Earth before, and sooner or later another will appear. We can only trust that when this happens, our ingenuity will be able to prevent catastrophe.

Getting hotter

Think of the world as a greenhouse. The glass walls and roof are the Earth's atmosphere, letting in the sunlight and trapping the heat to keep the inside warm. But there's a growing problem. Gases from fuels burnt off by industry, transport and deforestation are building up in the atmosphere, so that heat is escaping more slowly. This greenhouse effect is causing global warming, which is already a cause for alarm.

Climate zones today

Europe

Africa

Zones of the future?

Europe

Africa

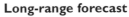

- Rainforest
- Sub-tropical (hot summer, mild winter)
- Desert
- Temperate (warm summer, cold winter)
- Savannah
- Sub-arctic

Long-range forecast

If global warming continues, the polar ice caps could melt, and climate zones across the world will move northwards. In the latitudes of Europe, for example, cool countries such as France, Germany and Britain would become sub-tropical. Sunny Spain and Italy would be scorched into deserts, and hot, dry North Africa would turn into a vast expanse of grassy savannah.

Paris in the heat

In the future, could northern cities such as Paris be sweltering in sub-tropical weather? Yes, say some experts, if global warming causes a shift in world climate belts. While northern regions might welcome warmer weather, the possible effect on agriculture could be calamitous. The world's cereal-growing regions could turn into deserts, leading to mass famine. Global warming could make changes to rainfall patterns too. Regions with regular rain year-round may soon face monsoon-like downpours that cause disastrous floods. If nothing else, the world will begin to look very different. The pyramids of Egypt, for example, would no longer stand in dry desert sands, but in green grasslands.

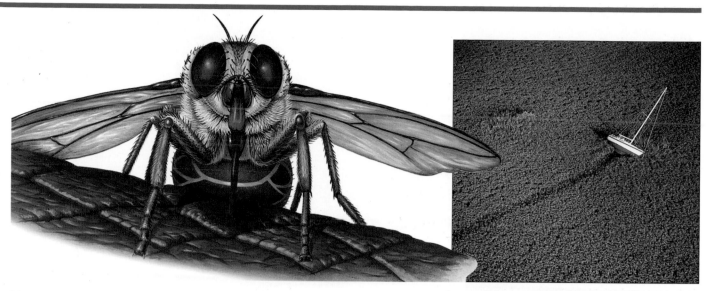

Unwelcome visitors

Temperatures may rise by as much as three degrees centigrade during the next 100 years – five times the rise during the last. This would enable warm-climate plant and wildlife species to migrate north, perhaps bringing unwelcome visitors such as the deadly tsetse fly and malarial mosquito to parts of Europe and the United States, where these insects have never been a threat before.

Building up a storm

Global warming is blamed for an increase in the number of violent storms. Hurricanes such as Mitch, which devastated Central America in 1998, are said to have become 40 percent more frequent since 1970.

World under water

If our planet continues to warm up, we could all be in deep trouble. Water expands as it heats, so the oceans would rise and threaten coastlines. There is a danger, too, that the polar ice caps may gradually melt as temperatures increase. Some scientists predict that the combined effect could cause a catastrophic rise in sea levels by the end of the 21st century. Without flood defences in place, that would put major cities at risk in many heavily populated regions of the world.

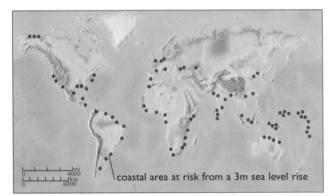

coastal area at risk from a 3m sea level rise

Disappearing from the map

Some scientists have estimated that sea levels could rise three metres by the year 2100. If this happens, dozens of coastal belts, including major cities such as Bangkok, St Petersburg and New Orleans, would face disastrous flooding. Whole regions including southern Florida in the USA, much of the Netherlands and half of Bangladesh would be awash. The areas at risk account for one third of the world's vital crop-growing land.

Mind the gap

Pollution causes more danger than global warming. Chemicals called CFCs – used, for example, in aerosols – drifted up into the sky for decades, destroying the ozone layer, the part of the Earth's atmosphere that protects us from cancer-causing

ultraviolet sunlight. The risk was ignored, until a huge hole was detected in the ozone layer over Antarctica in 1987. CFCs are now controlled, but too late to prevent this grave environmental disaster.

Wet outlook

The prospect of coastal cities such as New York sheltering behind sea walls in centuries to come is real. In the last 100 years, the average sea level has risen by 10–25cm, and the United Nations forecasts that it will rise four times faster in the 21st century. Ocean currents will cause much greater rises in some regions, threatening coastlines in future centuries with tides three to five metres higher than present levels – even without the extra hazard of melting polar ice caps.

Against the tide

The Thames Barrier, which was completed in 1984, protects London from the dangerous high tides that began to flood the city in the 20th century. The main gates, which each weigh 3,700 tonnes, close into a wall as high as a five-storey building. The barrier had to be raised 90 times in its first 20 years.

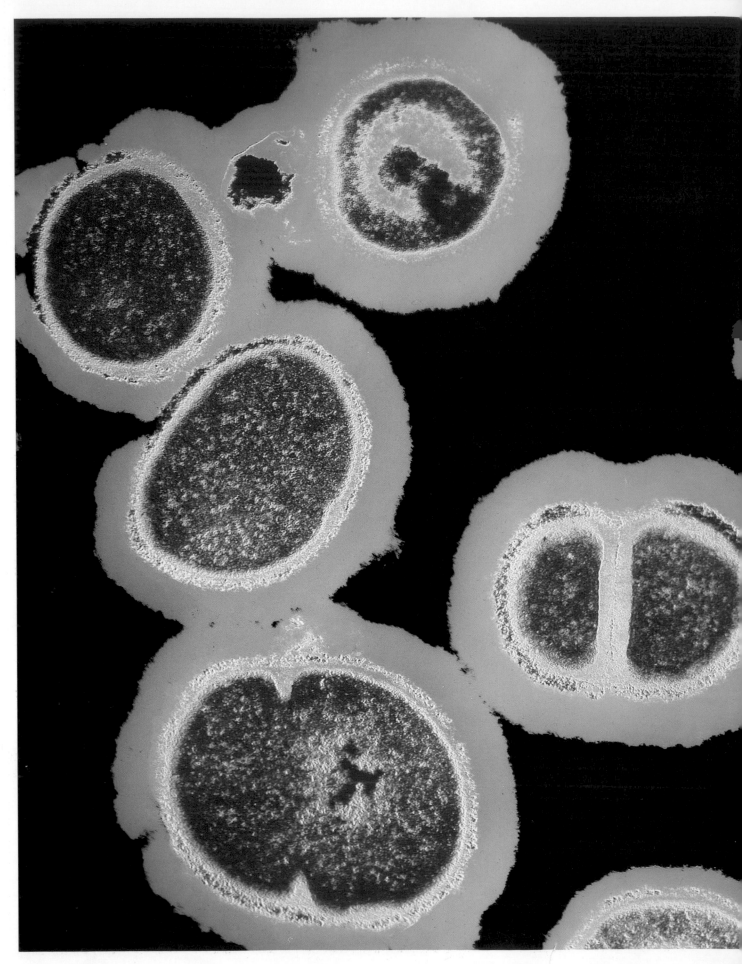

Medical threats

Our most dangerous enemies are invisible. In spite of medicine's amazing progress in the 20th century, microscopic monsters continue to stalk us. Deadly new viral diseases such as AIDS and Ebola have no known cure so far. And infectious bacteria, responsible for killers such as diphtheria and tuberculosis, are staging a comeback too. They have begun to develop resistance to antibiotics, the miracle drugs that doctors once hoped would consign them to history.

Risky business
To find new treatments for infectious diseases, researchers test thousands of different chemicals, one by one, on samples of the bacteria that cause them. It is a time-consuming task, and often a hazardous one. Testing deadly germs calls for extreme care and special precautions.

Survival expert
MRSA – Methicillin-resistant Staphylococcus Aureus – is a 'superbug' which even powerful antibiotics cannot destroy. The bacterium lives in hospitals, where it attacks – and kills – patients who have had operations. Pictured (*left*) at 500,000 times its actual size, MRSA is so dangerous that some hospitals refuse to admit patients who have the infection. Scientists are developing drugs to combat MRSA, but these miniscule organisms learn to change their form and behaviour just as quickly as new drugs appear. Their struggle to survive is as determined as that of any other life form.

Ancient remedy
In the search for cures, medicine turns to some surprising sources. A powerful new treatment for malaria, which kills millions each year, is based on a 2,000-year-old Chinese herbal remedy, and taken from the common plant family *Artemisia*.

Persistent killer
New diseases pose a constant threat of disastrous epidemics. In Africa, millions live in fear of the Ebola virus, named after a deadly outbreak in the Ebola River region of Zaire in 1976. One sufferer was transferred to the capital, Kinshasa, where the disease was found to be new – and infectious enough to threaten the city's two million people. The hospital, and the Ebola region, were instantly sealed off. The fever kills up to 90 percent of its victims and cannot be cured. It broke out again in 1995, killing most of the staff and patients at a hospital in Kikwit, Zaire. So infectious is the virus that even burial parties must wear protective clothing.

Crowded planet

Thanks to 20th-century technology, we live longer, travel further and produce more goods. We also multiply. There are now six billion of us, four times the number 100 years ago. We run a billion motor vehicles on our roads and consume more and more of the Earth's resources. In another century, there could be 15 billion people, all in need of jobs, homes, food, healthcare and transport. Unless growth slows, the world could be overwhelmed.

Population explosion

The United Nations hopes people will learn to limit children to two per couple. Population growth next century will depend on when this target is reached. The graph shows three possibilities. The highest figure is the likeliest, and could well be exceeded.

13 bn
12 bn
11 bn
10 bn
9 bn
8 bn
7 bn
6 bn
5 bn
4 bn
3 bn
2 bn
1 bn

1600   1700   1800   1900   2000   2100

Two children per family not reached until 2065. World population is 14.2 billion in 2100.

Two children per family not reached until 2035. World population is 11 billion in 2100.

Two children per family reached by 2010. Population is 7.5 billion in 2100.

The world's population today is over 6.3 billion.

From 1600–1900, the world's population grew slowly from 0.6 billion to 1.6 billion.

Key disadvantages
- Computers have revolutionized many activities, but our growing dependence on them may lead to problems in the future.
- Software 'bugs' threaten vital systems such as air-traffic control and defence.
- Users are desk-bound and can suffer from lack of personal contact.
- Children may become addicted to games, damaging their health and education.

Chaos in the streets

The city of the future is a crowded, nightmare vision. Dirty, traffic-choked streets and pavements are squeezed between high-rise buildings, in which solitary workers sit all day at computers in sound-proofed, sealed offices. Some cities are, of course, just like this now, but it is going to get much worse. Britain, for example, already has one of the world's most overcrowded road networks, with 100 vehicles for every kilometre. With car use growing at its present rate, there will be 50 percent more traffic by 2030. This dependence on cars will cause yet more problems of congestion, accidents and pollution.

Throwaway society

European households each throw out a tonne of rubbish every year. In the USA, it is even more. Disposal by burying or burning damages the environment – and the problem gets worse as people worldwide generate more and more waste.

Uncontrolled spread
Populations in the industrialized nations of Europe and North America are growing slowly, but in the developing world, high birth-rates double some countries' numbers every 20–30 years. Millions flock to cities, hoping to share the benefits of the consumer society. The many who find no work face a grim life in shanty towns such as those of Rio de Janeiro in Brazil (*left*) – already overcrowded and beset by poverty and disease.

San Francisco earthquake

Had the founders of San Francisco been warned, back in 1776, that they were building in one of the most dangerous places on Earth, they might well have decided to go elsewhere. But no warnings came, and San Francisco grew to be a vast and flourishing city. Yet it is placed almost directly above the San Andreas fault, the unstable intersection of two moving plates in the Earth's crust, and today's inhabitants know they could be struck, any time, by the kind of massive earthquake that destroyed the city in 1906.

Seconds from catastrophe

How much damage will a severe local earthquake do to San Francisco? The city had a disturbing foretaste in October 1989. An 11-second shock, only a tenth of the magnitude of the great 1906 quake, caused $6 billion in damage, made 12,000 people homeless and toppled an elevated section of highway, killing 42 motorists. Had the earthquake lasted the normal 20 to 30 seconds, thousands more buildings and roads would have been destroyed.

Shaken but undeterred

Just after 5am on 16 April 1906, San Francisco's half-million people were shaken awake by a terrifying earthquake. Buildings and roads collapsed, but the main damage came from the fires, started by gas leaks, which ravaged the city for three days. More than 700 people died and most of the city was destroyed. Afterwards, some citizens said it would be crazy to rebuild the city where it was sure, some day, to be struck again. But within three years, the central district had been completely restored – with new roads, bridges and buildings, all capable of withstanding severe shock and resisting fire. The San Francisco Bay Area now has ten times the population of a century ago.

shear walls reinforced with steel

central core contains lifts and stairs

cross-bracing strengthens structure

steel frame needs no core

joins are welded for immense strength

shock resistant foundations are made of steel and rubber

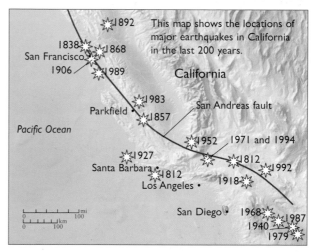

This map shows the locations of major earthquakes in California in the last 200 years.

California

San Andreas fault

Pacific Ocean

San Francisco
1892
1838
1868
1906
1989
Parkfield
1983
1857
1952
1971 and 1994
1927
Santa Barbara
1812
Los Angeles
1812
1918
1992
San Diego
1968
1987
1940
1979

Built to last

To prevent collapse during severe earthquakes, many modern buildings are cage-like structures formed round a strong central core. 'Shear' (one-piece) reinforced concrete walls and outer walls 'cross-braced' with diagonal beams provide support. Some buildings have steel frames welded into a single rigid structure – this needs less internal strengthening.

Danger zone

The San Andreas fault, extending 1,200km through California, is the meeting-point of two sections of the Earth's crust, the Pacific and North American plates. Earthquakes, caused by the plates grinding against each other, happen regularly here. There has been a major one about every ten years for the last two centuries.

Well prepared

The town of Parkfield lies on the San Andreas fault in a region of California hit by huge quakes in 1857 and 1983. It is now said to be the most intensely earthquake-monitored place in the world. The town's school is built to resist violent tremors, with shatter-proof windows and all heavy items from bookcases to computers bolted down. Pupils have earthquake drills at least once a month.

Meteorite!

Is bombardment from outer space pure science fiction? Not at all, according to scientists. The Earth is scarred by hundreds of impact sites. They include a crater carved by the meteorite probably responsible for the extinction of the dinosaurs 65 million years ago, and the vast area of Siberia obliterated by an exploding fireball as recently as 1908. No single death has been officially attributed to a space object – so far. How long will our luck hold?

Big hole
The Meteor Crater in Arizona, USA, provides unmistakable evidence that a huge object crashed into the Earth 50,000 years ago. To create such a pit, 1.3km wide and 175m deep, the meteorite must have been 40m wide, weighing 300,000 tonnes, and travelling at more than 48,000km/h.

Crash course

Asteroids, small planets orbiting the Sun, range from 1,000km-wide giants to tiny rock and iron fragments. When these objects hit Earth, we call them meteorites. The Earth collides harmlessly with small debris every day, nearly all of which is burnt up in the atmosphere, but if a big object struck, it could create worldwide devastation. Scientists estimate the chances of impact with such a meteorite at once every million years. Even so, they now constantly monitor space, because it could come at any time. It is only a slight comfort that an incoming object could possibly be intercepted by nuclear weapons to divert it from collision with Earth.

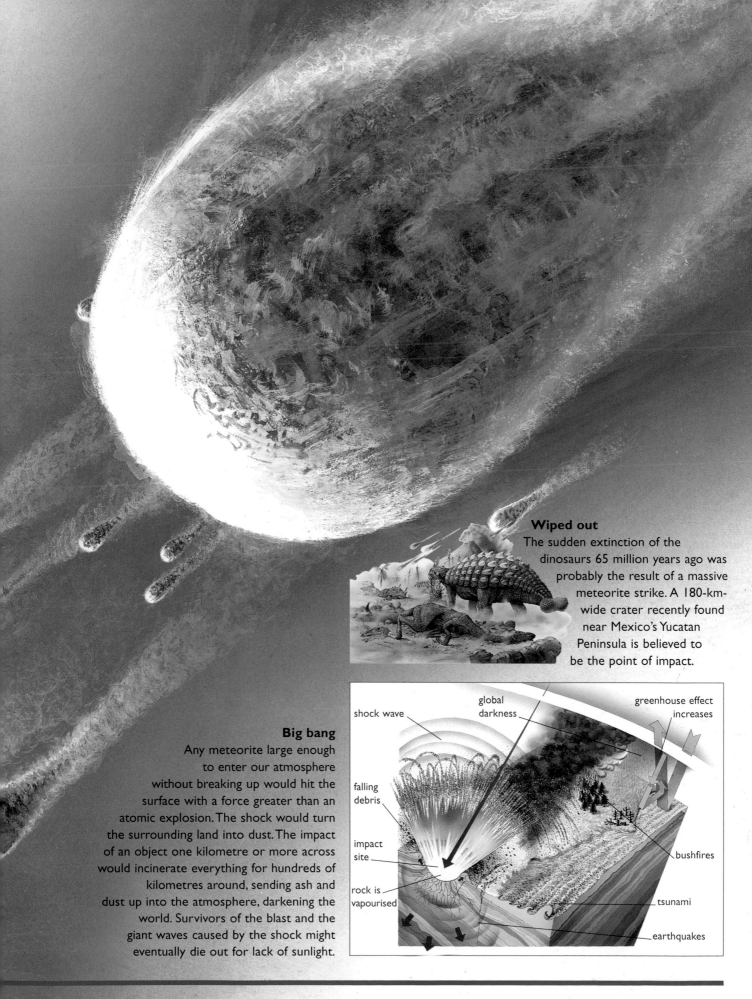

Wiped out

The sudden extinction of the dinosaurs 65 million years ago was probably the result of a massive meteorite strike. A 180-km-wide crater recently found near Mexico's Yucatan Peninsula is believed to be the point of impact.

Big bang

Any meteorite large enough to enter our atmosphere without breaking up would hit the surface with a force greater than an atomic explosion. The shock would turn the surrounding land into dust. The impact of an object one kilometre or more across would incinerate everything for hundreds of kilometres around, sending ash and dust up into the atmosphere, darkening the world. Survivors of the blast and the giant waves caused by the shock might eventually die out for lack of sunlight.

shock wave

global darkness

greenhouse effect increases

falling debris

impact site

rock is vapourised

bushfires

tsunami

earthquakes

Glossary

AIDS Acquired immune deficiency syndrome, a fatal illness caused by HIV (human immunodeficiency virus). Sufferers lose resistance to infections.

antibiotics Drugs made to combat bacteria.

asteroid A small rocky object orbiting the Sun. Collisions between asteroids, or a large planet's gravitational pull, cause some to change orbit and collide with Earth.

Atlantis In Ancient Greek legend, a great civilization that was lost under the sea.

bacteria Single-celled organisms, some of which cause infectious diseases. Most can be controlled with antibiotic drugs.

bubonic plague An infectious bacterial disease, named after the 'buboes' (swellings) under victims' skin. Also called the Black Death.

bushfire Fires in open country-side, often caused by drought, lightning strikes or arson.

carbon The element in fossil fuels, such as coal or oil, which gives off heat energy when burned.

carbon monoxide Poisonous gas given off by the burning of fossil fuels, such as coal or petrol, to generate heat or power.

CFCs Chlorofluorocarbons, the gases used in aerosols and fridges. The release of CFCs into the air causes destructive chemical reactions in the ozone layer.

delta The coastal region where a great river approaches the sea. The land around is formed of fertile silt.

diphtheria An infectious bacterial disease affecting the throat. It causes acute difficulties in breathing and swallowing.

dyke A long continuous mound raised on either side of a river to contain flooding.

ecosystem A community of living organisms. Each part of the system depends on others, and destruction of any single part of the system affects the rest.

epicentre The point on the Earth's surface directly above the source of an earthquake, from which the tremors radiate out.

fault line The joins between the mobile plates that make up the Earth's surface.

firebreak In firefighting, a space created by clearing away vegetation or buildings. The fire is unable to cross the gap.

fission In nuclear physics, the splitting of the component parts of atoms to produce energy.

fissure A crack in the ground caused by an earthquake or by volcanic activity.

flood-plain The low-lying region around a river or along a coastline where flooding is common.

greenhouse effect The heating of the Earth's atmosphere by pollution from burning fuels. The atmosphere naturally holds in the Sun's life-giving heat, but pollution is now preventing the heat from escaping as quickly as before. This is causing world temperatures to rise – the process of 'global warming'.

hoppers In the locust life-cycle, young insects with well-developed legs, but without wings.

hydro-electricity Electricity produced by water rushing from a dam's channels to turn turbines in a power station.

inflation The loss of money's value. If prices rise so that an item priced at £1 in January costs £1.10 in December, inflation is 10 percent. If the price rises from £1 to, say, £100 or more, that's hyperinflation.

latitude On a map, the distance north or south, from the equator. Thus, New York, Madrid, Rome and Beijing are on approximately the same latitude.

lava Molten rock that pours from a volcano in an eruption.

magma The super-hot liquid layer of rock in the Earth's crust.

meteorite A fragment of an asteroid that penetrates the Earth's atmosphere and collides with the surface.

Minoan Civilization An early nation on the island of Crete.

monsoon A seasonal wind in southern Asia which brings torrential rains each year.

nuclear power The harnessing of nuclear fission to generate electricity.

nutrients The substances in foods which provide nourishment.

ozone A gas in the atmosphere which absorbs much of the ultraviolet light in the Sun's rays.

pandemic A disease epidemic that spreads across the world.

plates Huge moving sections of the Earth's crust that lie beneath continents and oceans.

potato blight A destructive and fast-spreading disease caused by fungus. It breaks down potatoes into a brackish mush.

pyroclastic flow A dense cloud of burning rock, ash and gases that rolls down the sides of some erupting volcanoes at enormous speeds.

radioactive Atomic materials such as uranium exist in a constant state of nuclear disintegration and consequently emit radioactivity – which is fatal in large doses.

seismic Relating to earthquakes.

shares To raise money in order to expand their businesses, major companies issue shares. Each share represents a proportion of the company's value. Investors buy the shares in the hope that they will increase in value.

shock wave A sudden violent change in air pressure caused by an explosion, earthquake or massive movement such as a landslide.

silt The loose sand and earth carried by rivers and deposited across flood-plains.

stockbroker To buy or sell shares, investors use stockbrokers – people licensed to make transactions on the world's stock markets.

stock market Most large companies are 'publicly owned', which means that their shares can be bought by anyone on what is called the stock market. To buy or sell shares, investors use the stock exchanges which have been established in most nations.

sulphur dioxide A poisonous gas produced by burning fuels.

tenant A householder or farmer who pays rent to the landlord for the use of property or land.

tornado Violent winds whirling in a funnel-shaped formation.

tsunami Giant sea waves caused by undersea earthquakes or volcanoes.

tuberculosis A bacterial disease of the lungs.

turbine A propeller-like engine turned by water, steam, gas or wind to generate electricity.

ultraviolet Hazardous radiation in sunlight. It is filtered by the ozone layer.

United Nations An association of all the world's recognised nations dedicated to maintaining peace and human welfare.

uranium A mineral element used as a source of nuclear energy.

virus A microscopic organism that survives by invading a host animal or human. It causes disease as it multiplies in the body. Viruses cannot by killed by antibiotics.

vortex The spinning effect of rapidly circulating air which forms a tornado.

Index

Acknowledgements

The publishers would like to thank the following
illustrators for their contributions to this book:

b = bottom, c = centre, l = left, r = right, t = top, m = middle

Marion Appleton 5 *tr;* **T James Bayley** 2 *tr,* 19 *tl,* 26 *bl,* 27 *br,* 30, 35 *tr,* 36–37 *b,* 38 *ml,* 40 *cl,* 42 *bl,* 53 *tr,*
54 *bl, cl,* 56, 62 *tr;* **Julian Baum** 46 *t,* 62 *tl;* **Stephen Conlin** 7 *bl;* **Richard Draper** 3 *tl,* 14 *m,* 17 *tr,* 23 *m,*
25 *t,* 28 *bl,* 31 *t, c,* 34 *t,* 36 *tl,* 37 *t,* 42 *c,* 54 *t,* 57 *cl,* 59 *br,* 60 *tr,* 61 *tc, bl;* **David Farren** 2 *bl,* 15, 19 *b,* 20 *tl, bl,*
21 *t,* 24–25 *b,* 28 *tl,* 29, 44 *t, br,* 45 *bl,* 55, 64; **Chris Forsey** 4 *tl,* 5 *br,* 59 *cr;* **Nicholas Forder** 7, 13 *tr;*
Haywood Art Group 60 *cl;* **Christian Hook** 3 *tr,* 9 *tr,* 39 *tl;* **Michael Johnson** 1, 12–13 *b,* 34–35 *b,* 43,
50–51; **Maltings Partnership** 6 *br,* 11 *tl,* 47 *c,* 60 *bc,* 61 *br;* **Simon Mendez** 3 *b,* 8, 10–11 *b,* 14 *bl,* 16,
18 *bl,* 22 *b,* 32–33 *b,* 33 *t,* 38 *br,* 39 *b,* 48 *bl,* 49 *b,* 53 *bc,* 58–59, 62 *br, bl,* 63 *b;* **Eric Robson** 40 *tl;*
Jon Rogers 41; **M Taylor** 49 *tl;* 63 *cr*

The publishers would also like to thank the following
for supplying photographs for this book:

b = bottom, c = centre, l = left, r = right, t = top

Pages: **4** *bl* Planet Earth Pictures; **6** *cl* Rex Features/Sipa Press; **9** *c* Corbis UK/Sean Sexton Collection, *cr*
Robert Harding Picture Library/Adam Woolfitt; **11** *tr* Rex Features/Iwasa; **13** *tl* Corbis UK/Reuter; **14** *tl*
Rex Features/Hojciech Dadej; **17** *br* Rex Features/Houston Post/Sipa/Michael Boddy; **18** *tl* Rex
Features/Sipa; **21** *br* ET Archive/Bibliotheque Nationale; **23** *br* Rex Features/Blondin; **25** *cr*
Popperfoto/Reuters; **26** *br* Corbis UK; **28** *br* Still Pictures/Hartmut Schwarzbach; **31** *bc* Rex Features; **32** *tr*
FirePix International; **35** *tl* Popperfoto/UPI; **37** *cr* Mary Evans Picture Library; **38** *tr* Still Pictures/Al Grillo;
40 *bl* Popperfoto/Jason Reed/Reuters, *br* Popperfoto/Mazlan Enjah/Reuter; **42** *br* Popperfoto; **45** *cr* Corbis
UK/Bettmann/UPI; **47** *tr* Robert Harding Picture Library; *br* Still Pictures/Mark Carwardine; **49** *tr* Tony
Stone Images/Cameron Davidson; **51** *tr* Still Pictures/Mark Edwards; **52** Science Photo Library/Dr Kari
Lounatmaa; **53** *cr* Popperfoto/Reuters/Corinne Dufka; **55** *tl* Still Pictures/John Maier; **56** *tl* Popperfoto; **57** *br*
Science Photo Library/David Parker; **58** *tr* Galaxy Picture Library/David Brown

*Every effort has been made to trace the copyright holders of the photographs.
The publishers apologise for any inconvenience caused.*